☜ **W9-BSQ-353**

DATE DUE

~~9-29-09~~	~~9-29-09~~		
~~9/3~~	~~9-29-09~~		
~~8-6-2000~~			
~~3/1/06~~			
~~			
~~12-2-08~~			
~~11-20-08~~			
~~12-1-08~~			
~~1/5/09~~			
~~12-3-09~~			

Freeman, C.
   Horse trainer (A Day in
the life of a horse
trainer)

DEMCO

A DAY IN THE LIFE OF A
Horse Trainer

by Charlotte McGuinn Freeman
Photography by Gayle Jann

Troll Associates

Library of Congress Cataloging in Publication Data

Freeman, Charlotte McGuinn.
   A day in the life of a horse trainer.

     Summary: Follows a horse trainer through her day
as she exercises the horses, teaches riding, prepares
both horse and rider for competition, and participates
herself in competitive events.
     [1. Horse trainers—Juvenile literature. 2. Show
horses—Training—Juvenile literature. 3. Lenehan,
Leslie—Juvenile literature. 4. Horsemen and
horsewomen—United States—Juvenile literature.
[1. Horse trainers. 2. Horsemanship. 3. Occupations.
4. Lenehan, Leslie] I. Jann, Gayle, ill. II. Title.
SF285.25.F74   1988   636.1'088   87-10681
ISBN 0-8167-1111-9 (lib. bdg.)
ISBN 0-8167-1112-7 (pbk.)

Leslie Lenehan is a horse trainer. She trains both horses and riders, and competes in many events at horse shows all over the country. She is a World Cup champion and a member of the United States Equestrian Team, which competes in the Olympic Games. She has been riding horses and competing at horse shows since she was a child.

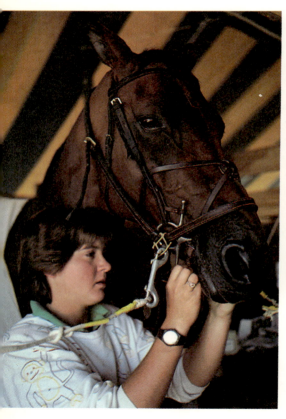

By caring for the horses, grooms make it possible for the trainers and riders to concentrate on each event in the competition. One of Leslie's grooms adjusts the horse's bridle so the fitting will not irritate the horse's mouth. Grooms work out of grooming stalls, where they can keep all their tools within easy reach.

The day begins early for everyone at a horse show. The grooms who feed and take care of the horses arrive before dawn. As the sun rises, they are already at work exercising their horses. For one exercise, the groom holds the end of a long rein, called a "lunge line," while the horse moves in circles around her.

Both horse and rider must warm up their stiff muscles before competition begins. Like athletes, show horses must practice their skills over and over. It is a horse trainer's job to teach the horse these skills. After spending the night in its stall, the horse also needs a chance in the morning to work off excess energy.

Young horses are very strong and often a little wild, so it is important for them to be properly trained. Horse trainers like Leslie often work with horses that belong to other people. They train them so even less-experienced riders can control the horse and compete safely.

One of the grooms asks Leslie which bridle to put on the next horse. The horse and rider who work best as a team have the best chance for success in this sport. Leslie rides many horses during a typical day. Some of them wear shin boots to protect their legs.

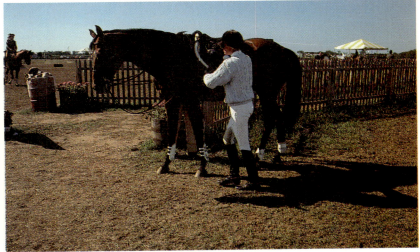

After a workout, Leslie dismounts and loosens the "girth," or strap that holds the saddle on the horse's back. Now the horse will be more comfortable. Basic grooming and care of the horse are some of the first skills beginning riders learn. Taking good care of the horse is an important part of good horsemanship.

It takes a lot of work to prepare a horse for competition. The horse's mane and tail must be braided, for in many events the horse will be judged on appearance as well as performance. Braiders arrive at two or three o'clock in the morning to get all their horses braided in time for the competition.

A "farrier" is a blacksmith who works specifically with horses. The skills of this trade are often passed down from one family member to another through the generations. Pounding a red hot horseshoe into shape, the farrier forms a specially designed shoe that will support a horse's weak hoof.

The farrier fits the hot horseshoe to the horse's hoof. Then he will take it off and see where it has burned the hoof. The unburned spots will show where the shoe fits incorrectly. Horses' hooves are made of the same substance as our fingernails, so this process does not hurt the horse.

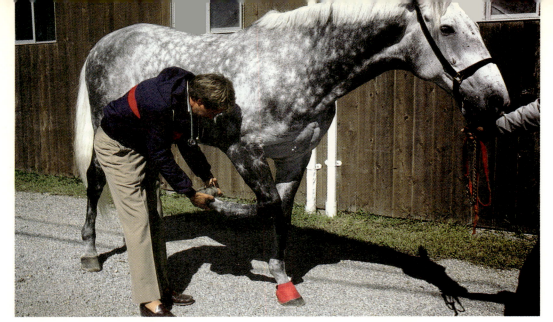

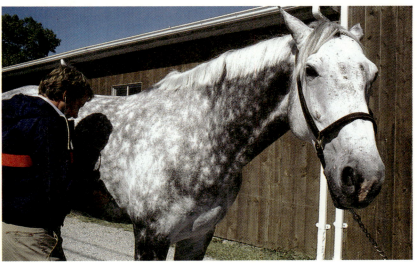

When horses jump, their legs are under great stress. If an injury occurs, a veterinarian will check the horse's hoof and leg. The vet may also listen to the horse's heart, to make sure the horse is healthy. Horses sometimes wear "bell boots" to protect their hooves from any knocks they may receive.

In the "schooling ring," or practice ring, Leslie sets the top rail for one of her students to use in her warm up. A second rail is placed on the ground as a guide to both the horse and rider. It will help indicate how far from the fence the horse should begin jumping in order to clear the top rail.

Leslie watches as the horse clears the fence. Then she rewards the horse for a job well done, and gives the rider a few pointers about the event coming up. Debbie is a promising young rider who has won a number of championships. She listens carefully to each suggestion Leslie makes.

Leslie checks the bulletin board. This is where the course diagram and "order of go" are posted. Riders study the course diagram and discuss the best approaches for the different kinds of fences. Some fences are very broad, while others are high. Some fences have water beneath them, while others are placed close together in combination.

Jumping courses are designed to challenge horse and rider both physically and mentally. Leslie tells her students how to approach each hazard. Some jumps have double rails on top of a "stone" wall. The rails are attached loosely, so they will fall if a horse fails to clear the jump.

Other hazards have water hidden on the opposite side of the fence. Before each event, the riders walk the entire course to examine the hazards and to pace off the distance between fences. This helps them to judge the number of "strides," or steps, the horse should take between jumps.

Everyone springs into action as the event begins. A groom touches up the horse's hooves with hoof dressing so they will look dark and shiny. Meanwhile, Leslie gives Debbie some important last-minute tips and encouragement before she enters the ring. It is important for each rider to remain calm and focused in order to compete successfully.

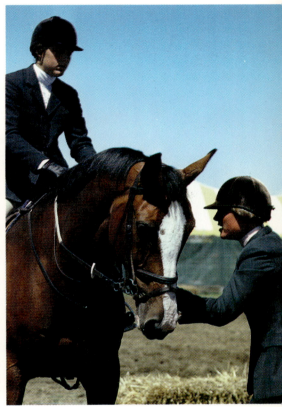

Leslie will also compete in this event, but first she watches Debbie's performance. Debbie barely clears a large "brick" wall. These fences are difficult to jump because they are high and look solid. Actually, they are built from blocks that are very light and easily knocked down.

Leslie waits in the "in-gate" until it is her turn to go. Then she enters the ring. In order to win, Leslie must clear all the fences in the quickest time. Her time for this event will begin when she passes through the electric eye of a timer. The top forty horses in this event will qualify to compete in the Grand Prix.

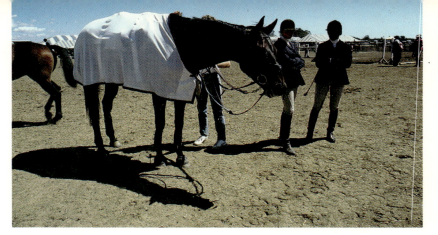

After the event is over, Leslie and Debbie discuss their performances while waiting for the results to be announced. Debbie won a red ribbon for second place in this event. Although Leslie did not win a ribbon, she has qualified to ride in the Grand Prix, the most important event of the day.

Back at the barns, a horse who will not compete again today is washed down. After competition, each horse is soaped, rinsed and scraped down with a special tool so his coat dries faster. This keeps the horse's coat shiny and clean. Then the horse will be covered with a light blanket and put back in its stall.

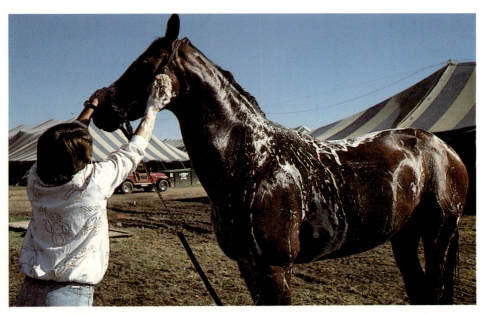

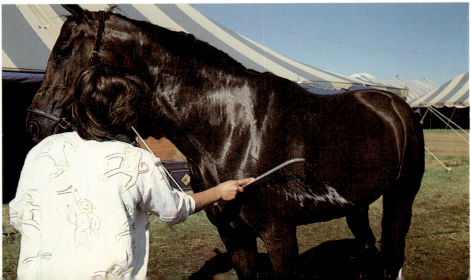

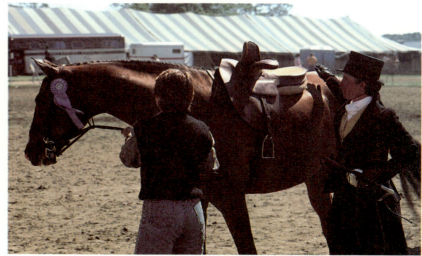

One of Leslie's students competes in the sidesaddle class. Until this century, women always rode sidesaddle, with both legs on the same side of the horse. Today few people ride this way, and sidesaddle events are becoming rare. Leslie's student wins the blue ribbon in this difficult event.

Everyone is busy preparing for the Grand Prix.
In this event, the horses must jump large fences
very quickly. The horse who has the fastest time
and who knocks down the fewest rails wins the
event. Workers put finishing touches on some of
the jumps as Conrad Holmfeld, the course de-
signer, checks a fence.

Leslie puts on her Olympic Team jacket. Only members of the Olympic Team can wear this scarlet jacket with the team insignia and the blue-and-white collar. Leslie was a member of the first American Olympic team ever to win the gold medal—at the 1984 games in Los Angeles.

As Leslie enters the ring to compete, she must concentrate on the course ahead of her. She cannot allow the crowds to distract her or her horse. Leslie has competed many times in front of crowds, and has learned to focus her attention on the task before her.

Leslie and her horse, Siriska, ride the entire course without knocking any fences down. This is called a clear round. Although their time is not as fast as the times of some of the other horses, their clear round on this difficult course has placed them high in the standings.

Riders score points in Grand Prix events like these throughout the year to qualify for the World Cup Championships. After receiving a white fifth place ribbon, Leslie congratulates one of her Olympic teammates. Then she and Debbie ride out of the ring together. Debbie won eighth place in the event.

Leslie and Siriska pose for photographs with the ribbon they have won. Leslie signs autographs and accepts congratulations from Siriska's owners. Most of the horses Leslie rides belong to people who are not riders themselves. The sport could not go on without owners and patrons who help with the expenses of national competition.

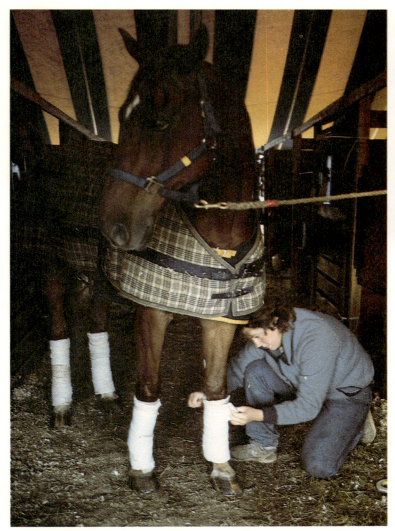

After two weeks of competition, the show is over. The grooms bandage the horses' legs to protect them during the van ride. Then the horses are loaded on the big eight-horse vans. They usually move from one horse show straight to the next. This time, they will have a week at their home barn before moving on to the next show.

Horse trainers get up before dawn and work long, hard days. They spend many months of the year on the road competing in sun and rain, dust and mud. They do it because of their love and respect for horses, the friendship of the people on the circuit, and the challenge and thrill of competition.